Pirates

by Jim Brew

BELLWETHER MEDIA · MINNEAPOLIS, MN

TM

Are you ready to take it to the extreme?
Torque books thrust you into the action-packed world
of sports, vehicles, mystery, and adventure. These books
may include dirt, smoke, fire, and dangerous stunts.
Warning: read at your own risk.

Library of Congress Cataloging-in-Publication Data

Brew, Jim.
 Pirates / by Jim Brew.
   p. cm. -- (Torque: history's greatest warriors)
 Includes bibliographical references and index.
 Summary: "Engaging images accompany information about pirates. The combination of high-interest
subject matter and light text is intended for students in grades 3 through 7"--Provided by publisher.
 ISBN 978-1-60014-747-0 (hardcover : alk. paper)
 1. Pirates--Juvenile literature. I. Title.
 G535.B74 2012
 910.4'5--dc23   2011031241

This edition first published in 2012 by Bellwether Media, Inc.

Printed in the United States of America, North Mankato, MN.

010112   1202

Contents

Who Were Pirates?

In the 1600s and early 1700s, no sight was more feared than a pirate ship. Pirates sailed the seas in search of victims. They would capture ships to steal valuables. Then they would keep the ships or sink them. Sailors were sometimes killed or left on a **desert island**.

Pirate Fact

Some pirate ships flew
plain black or red flags.
Others featured a white
skull and crossbones on a
black background. This was
called the "Jolly Roger."

The most famous pirates sailed the Caribbean Sea. Blackbeard, Henry Morgan, and other pirates **terrorized** all who entered their territory. They used clever **tactics** and powerful ships to prey on **trade ships**. The speed of pirate ships allowed them to **evade** the warships of European navies.

Blackbeard

Henry Morgan

Pirate Skills

Pirates had no formal training. They were sailors looking for a way to get rich. Many pirates were former members of navies. Some left the navy for the promise of **plunder**. Others had lost their jobs with the navy and had nowhere else to turn. Their sailing skills made them valuable crew members aboard pirate ships.

Pirate Fact

Some countries hired pirates to harass enemy trade ships. These pirates were called privateers.

Pirate captains had to be excellent sailors and fighters. It was also important for them to know how to **navigate**. They had to know the location of popular **trade routes** and pirate **hideouts**. Crews would **mutiny** against captains who failed to lead them to plunder.

All pirates had to know how to use swords, knives, and guns. They learned to throw and climb ropes so they could easily move from ship to ship.

Pirate Equipment

flintlock
pistol

cutlass

The short, curved cutlass was the most common pirate sword. Some pirates also carried daggers and knives. The flintlock pistol was a handgun that pirates used to fire a single shot. The blunderbuss was a large, wide-barreled gun. A pirate would stuff a blunderbuss with **shot** or nails. One blast could take out many victims.

blunderbuss

Pirate Fact

Cannons aboard pirate ships could fire cannonballs up to 3,000 feet (914 meters)!

Pirate Fact

Pirates stole navigation tools from the ships they captured. They used the tools to travel the seas or sold them for money.

Pirates also needed equipment to capture ships. They threw boarding hooks onto the other ships so they could climb aboard. Some pirates carried boarding axes. These small axes had a blade on one end and a sharp **pike** on the other. They could be used to fight or climb.

boarding axe

boarding hook

Pirate Ships

The ultimate weapon of pirates was their ship. Pirates preferred ships that had a balance of speed and power. They had large sails to catch the wind and cannons to blast through other ships.

Brigantine

This large pirate ship stood up well in long battles. It had two masts to hold sails. It was fast, easy to maneuver, and could carry more than 100 pirates.

Galley

This long, narrow ship had oars as well as sails. This allowed it to come upon victims without any wind. A galley could carry more than 100 pirates.

Schooner

This ship had two or more masts to hold sails, making it very fast. It held up to 75 pirates and could travel in water as shallow as 5 feet (1.5 meters).

Sloop

The sloop was small and fast. It could move well in shallow water, even with the weight of 70 pirates and 15 cannons.

The Decline of Pirates

The late 1600s and early 1700s are called the Golden Age of Piracy. That was when Caribbean pirates were at their strongest. In the early 1700s, many nations set out to bring pirates to justice for their crimes. The deadliest enemy for pirates was Great Britain's Royal Navy. The Royal Navy sent many warships to the Caribbean to find and kill pirates.

Pirate Fact

Pirates still exist today in some parts of the world. Modern pirates have become a big problem on the east coast of northern Africa.

By the mid-1700s, many of the Caribbean's pirates had been captured or killed. In the early 1800s, the navies of the United States, Great Britain, and other nations fought to end piracy once and for all. They wiped out almost all of the remaining pirates. Only a few pirate ships were sailing by the late 1800s. Pirates were no longer the terror of the Caribbean Sea.

Glossary

desert island—an island not inhabited by people

evade—to stay away from

hideouts—secret, hidden bases

mutiny—to rise up against a superior; a pirate crew would mutiny to remove their captain as leader.

navigate—to find one's way in unfamiliar territory

pike—the sharp point of a boarding axe; pirates used the pike to climb aboard other ships.

plunder—money and property taken by force

shot—small balls of metal fired out of certain types of firearms

tactics—military strategies

terrorized—filled with fear

trade routes—routes commonly used by trade ships

trade ships—ships used to carry goods from place to place

To Learn More

AT THE LIBRARY

Hamilton, John. *A Pirate's Life*. Edina, Minn.: ABDO Pub. Co., 2007.

Harrison, David L. *Pirates*. Honesdale, Pa.: Wordsong, 2008.

Lewis, J. Patrick. *Blackbeard, The Pirate King: Several Yarns Detailing the Legends, Myths, and Real-life Adventures of History's Most Notorious Seaman*. Washington, D.C.: National Geographic Society, 2006.

ON THE WEB

Learning more about pirates is as easy as 1, 2, 3.

1. Go to www.factsurfer.com.

2. Enter "pirates" into the search box.

3. Click the "Surf" button and you will see a list of related Web sites.

With factsurfer.com, finding more information is just a click away.

Index

Great care has been taken to select images that are both historically accurate and engaging. The depictions of the warriors in this book may vary slightly due to the use of images from multiple sources and reenactments.